A souvenir guide

Chirk Castle

Wrexham

National Trust

We

Th

Welcome to Chirk

For many visitors, Chirk is just a castle; perhaps at a stretch a noble family home, but first and foremost a proud, medieval building that stands firm at the head of the Ceiriog Valley. Completed in 1310, Chirk was one of a string of 'Marcher fortresses' built during Edward I's reign to subdue the unruly Welsh and bring Wales firmly into the conquering monarch's kingdom.

Chirk was constructed for strategic reasons on land that, until 1282, belonged to the last princes of Wales. This borderland had for centuries witnessed violent struggles between the English and the Welsh. High on a rocky outcrop above the point where the rivers Dee and Ceiriog meet, the Castle was there to make a statement. Its lime-washed silhouette stood stark against the skyline: a brooding English presence in these disputed lands.

Symbol of power

As imposing as it is, there is much more to Chirk than its building. Today, the estate covers 195 hectares (481 acres), but in its early days it sprawled across thousands of acres, taking in whole villages, mines, woodland and farmland. For early owners, the Castle was not as important as the land and its lordship; without these, the Castle would have been unmanageable: a military millstone too expensive to maintain.

A hard-working land

The estate comprised a hunting park and agricultural land. The Myddelton family, who lived here for over 400 years, let much of the land to farmers. Nowadays the apparently bucolic location belies its industrial past. In the early 19th century, North Wales was a place of heavy industry; the Myddeltons owned copper, coal and lead mines, and an iron forge. Industrial structures built in the area were of breathtaking scale and ambition – so much so, in fact, that Chirk now looks out onto a World Heritage Site. The nearby aqueducts and canals by Thomas Telford and William Jessop to transport coal, granite, ore and slate were lauded for their innovation and classical elegance. And their design was influenced by Chirk itself: the Castle's then owner, Richard Myddelton, insisted that any such structures shouldn't spoil the aesthetic appeal of the Ceiriog Valley or any of the views across his recently landscaped estate. Telford and Jessop came up with a revolutionary cast-iron and stone aqueduct that created, as they'd hoped, 'a romantic feature in the view'.

Left A view of Chirk Castle from the north east

A rare and prized park

While the surrounding estate is a World Heritage Site, Chirk's medieval hunting park has its own distinction: it was a major part of Chirk Castle's designation as a Site of Special Scientific Interest in 2012.

The park has been continually managed for hundreds of years and this stability has been good for wildlife, allowing rare dead wood beetles, ancient trees, a colony of lesser horseshoe bats, grassland fungi and other rare flora and fauna to flourish. The Castle also stands within an Area of Outstanding Natural Beauty. Wild Welsh ponies graze, buzzards fly and hares leap, all within an ecosystem preserved by hundreds of years of one family's ownership.

Below The Lower Lawn and the Castle's east front in winter

Above Chirk Castle is as imposing from the air as it is from the ground

Landscaped gardens

The gardens make the most of the Castle's place within its broader landscape. Conceived as pleasure grounds, they offer stunning views over the Cheshire and Shropshire plains. They date back to the 18th century, when William Emes, a pupil of Lancelot 'Capability' Brown, was tasked with landscaping the garden and estate. His creation – a combination of ordered gardens and rolling landscape – was designed to underline the status and wealth of the Myddeltons.

All is not what it seems

Chirk straddles an ancient boundary between two warring countries. It is a family home, an agricultural estate, an ancient woodland, a home for rare animals and wildlife, and a lush pleasure ground whose formal gardens command breathtaking views. It borders a World Heritage Site, with its owners playing an important role in creating an industrial landscape of startling beauty and ingenuity. It is 700 years of English and Welsh history spread across acres of land in a myriad of unexpected and delightful ways.

The People of Chirk

During the medieval period, Chirk oscillated between glory and disgrace. Five of its owners were executed for treason, their estates seized by the Crown and their tenants caught in the crossfire of wars that rumbled on for centuries. Then, in 1595, the Myddelton family turned the fortress into a family home and occupied it continuously for the next 400 years.

Left Condemned to death by Queen Isabella, Hugh Despenser was hanged, castrated, drawn and quartered at Hereford on 24 November 1326

Above Queen Isabella and her troops at Hereford

Builder of the Castle: Roger Mortimer

Roger Mortimer (?1256–1326) came to royal attention during the Welsh rebellion in 1282. After the Welsh were subdued, Edward I gave Roger, captain of the English army, the land around Chirk. Construction on the Castle began in 1295.

In 1308, Edward II appointed Roger Justiciar of Wales and for the next 14 years Roger acted as a surrogate Prince of Wales. But ambition got the better of him. For years, there had been political tussling between the King's favourite, Hugh Despenser the Younger, and the barons jealous of the Despenser family's influence.

In the 'Despenser wars' that followed executions became regular, with infighting so dire that Edward II's wife, Queen Isabella, fled to France. In 1322, Roger Mortimer was persuaded to take up arms against the Despensers and the King. The gamble didn't pay off. Mortimer was thrown into the Tower of London and died there in 1326.

Loyalty and treason: Roger Mortimer of Wigmore

In the same year Roger Mortimer's nephew Roger Mortimer of Wigmore (1287–1330), escaped the Tower where he had been imprisoned alongside his uncle. He fled to France, joined Isabella and became her lover. While the Mortimers had been in the Tower, the King had given Chirk to the second Earl of Arundel. Returning to England, Isabella and Roger promptly captured and beheaded the latter.

Having regained his land, Roger then turned his attention to Hugh Despenser the Younger. The King's former favourite was hung, drawn and quartered and Edward II himself was forced to abdicate. Roger and Isabella ruled England for three years, but when the young Edward III came of age in 1330, he had Mortimer executed, on no less than 14 counts of treason.

Up, down and up again: Three Earls of Arundel

In 1335 Chirk was granted to the 3rd Earl of Arundel, Richard Fitzalan II (1313–76). One of the richest men in England, he spent large sums remodelling his principal home, Arundel Castle in Sussex. Despite carrying Richard II's crown at his coronation in 1377, Richard Fitzalan III, 4th Earl of Arundel (1346–97), was one of the Lords Appellants who took up arms against the King in 1388.

The King never forgave him and had the Earl beheaded. Richard went calmly to his death in 1397 and Chirk was taken from the Fitzalans, but the merry-go-round of political fighting meant the estate was soon back in their hands.

Richard Fitzalan's son Thomas sided with the future King Henry IV; when he ousted Richard II in 1399, Thomas got his castle back and went on to fight for Henry IV and later for Henry V during the Hundred Years War. This meant Chirk's revenues took as much of a battering as the King's men in France, although in the end it wasn't political strife or even penury that defeated Thomas Fitzalan. He contracted dysentery at the siege of Harfleur in 1415 and died shortly afterwards; he had no son, so Chirk Castle once again reverted to the Crown.

Below Effigies of Thomas Fitzalan and his wife Beatrice in the Fitzalan Chapel in the grounds of Arundel Castle

Above left Thomas Myddelton I

Above right Thomas Myddelton II

Chirk under the Tudors

In 1495, after Chirk's then owner Sir William Stanley had been executed for treason, the Crown held the estate for 50 years, rewarding royal officials with posts on the Chirk estates. In 1563, Elizabeth I gave the Castle to her favourite, Robert Dudley. After his death it passed through several hands until, on 14 August 1595, Chirk was sold for £5,000 to Thomas Myddelton and the Castle's story turned a new page.

The first of many: Sir Thomas Myddelton I

The younger son of the then-governor of Denbigh Castle, Sir Thomas (1550–1631) left Wales to make his fortune in London. He did so with remarkable success, investing in both the East India Company and the Virginia Company. He built a country seat in Essex, was knighted, and in 1613 became Lord Mayor of London. He also became Denbighshire's greatest landowner, developing copper mines at Neath, and loaning money to the local gentry. Today, his legacy lives on in the North Range at Chirk, which he built, and in his sponsorship of the first popular edition of the Bible in Welsh.

The Civil War general: Sir Thomas Myddelton II

Sir Thomas Myddelton II (1586–1666) was both political and religious, an MP and a Presbyterian. In 1642, as England broke apart under the divisive rule of Charles I, Sir Thomas urged his fellow countrymen to support Parliament. In 1643 the King ordered royalist neighbours to take over Chirk. A year later, Sir Thomas 'attempted to work into the Castle with iron crows and pickers under great planks and tables' but couldn't gain entry. Had he used artillery he could have succeeded, but he refused to bombard his own home. In the end, money did what military might could not: in 1646, Sir John Watts was bribed to abandon the Castle, and Sir Thomas Myddelton II

Above The Coronation Procession of Charles II on 22 April 1661

moved back in. The conflict dragged on, one civil war leading to two more; the King was beheaded and Oliver Cromwell presided over a military dictatorship. In 1651 the moderate and by now disillusioned Thomas began corresponding with the exiled Charles II.

Right Thomas Myddelton IV

In 1658, Cromwell died. A year later, in the political vacuum that followed, Sir Thomas backed Sir George Booth's Cheshire Rising and went to Wrexham market place to declare Charles II as king. When Booth was defeated, the Castle was again besieged, but this time by Parliamentarians. The east wall and towers at either end were torn down. The Castle lay in ruins.

When Charles II regained the throne in 1660, he restored the Myddeltons to Chirk. But it was ten years before they could repair their home and re-occupy it. Of all Edward I's marcher fortresses Chirk is the only one that is still inhabited today. We have Sir Thomas Myddelton II to thank for that.

The grieving husband and father: Thomas Myddelton IV

Sir Thomas III died in 1663, leaving a 12-year-old son to inherit Chirk. Thomas Myddelton IV (1651–84) was guided by the steady hand of his grandmother, Mary Napier, who after her husband's death ensured that Chirk's restoration continued. When Thomas came of age, he picked up the rebuilding reins, only to die aged just 32 with no surviving male heirs.

Politics and industry: Sir Richard Myddelton

In 1685 Sir Richard Myddelton (1655–1716) inherited Chirk. In the same year, he was elected MP for Denbighshire, a position he held for 32 years. Richard's other interests lay in hunting, horseracing and in his lucrative exploitation of coalmines at Black Park and an iron forge in the hamlet of Pont-y-blew. He commissioned the glorious Davies Gates (see page 55). Sir Richard was succeeded by his only son William and when the latter died two years later, Chirk passed to a cousin, Robert.

Brothers in arts: Robert and John Myddelton

The fruits of Sir Richard's labour allowed the next two Myddeltons to enjoy life as landed gentry to the full. Robert Myddelton (1678–1733) had the Davies Gates placed in front of the Castle and added monumental iron pillars on which sat two wolves – alluding to the family's ancestor, Ririd Flaidd, 'the Wolf'. He also commissioned the colossal statues of Mars and Hercules as well as a group of paintings by the celebrated painter, Peter Tillemans. When Robert died heirless, his brother and fellow patron of the arts, John (1685–1747) inherited the estate.

Left Richard Myddelton

Opposite Elizabeth Rushout

Left Robert Myddelton

Opposite Robert Myddelton Biddulph

Richard Myddelton and Elizabeth Rushout

Chirk become even more grandiose under John's son, Richard (1726–95), who married the wealthy heiress Elizabeth Rushout (?1730–72) of Northwick Park, Gloucestershire. In 1770, Elizabeth appointed the architect Joseph Turner of Chester to remodel the state rooms in a neoclassical style. While his wife focused on the interiors, Richard turned his attention to the estate. He appointed William Emes, a

pupil of 'Capability' Brown, to landscape the park and gardens. Emes swept away roads, walls and fences, opened up views across the Cheshire and Shropshire plains, and planted thousands of trees.

Charlotte Myddelton Biddulph and her son Robert

Richard Myddelton was outlived by his son by only a year, and with no other male heirs, the Myddelton estate was split in three. Richard's elder daughter, Charlotte (1770–1843), who married Robert Biddulph, inherited Chirk Castle and its immediate estate in 1796; Ruthin Castle went to Maria; and Harriet had the land around Wrexham. It was apparently an unhappy affair, with the trio squabbling over their inheritance. Some 25 years of legal wrangling were eventually settled by an Act of Parliament. At Chirk, Charlotte and Robert appointed Thomas Harrison of Chester in 1820 to create a suite of apartments in the East Range. Their son, Colonel Robert Myddelton Biddulph (1805–72), commissioned A.W.N. Pugin, the Gothic Revival genius, to make a grander 'medieval' castle than it had ever been before. This proved a far from straightforward task.

'Such a job as Chirk is enough to drive any man mad. All little things are as difficult to get done as the greatest.'

A.W.N. Pugin, 1846

The first to go public: Richard Myddelton

Despite the rising costs of running the estate, Richard (1837–1913) continued his father's building projects. He also opened the Castle to the public, but rather than using the entrance fees for the upkeep of the Castle, he generously donated them to charity. In 1911, Richard was forced to take drastic action: he auctioned off a huge swathe of land, as well as a number of buildings and much of the Castle's contents, and put the Castle itself up for rent.

The influential tenant: Thomas Scott-Ellis

While motoring through North Wales in 1910, Thomas Scott-Ellis (1880–1946), 8th Lord Howard de Walden, fell in love with the landscape. The following year Tommy, as he was known, took a 35-year lease on the Castle. A man of many talents, his personal interests ranged from writing plays and libretti for operas to commissioning flying machines and supplying the British army with radio communications. He established the Welsh National Theatre, was an accomplished military man and also a brilliant sportsman, even competing in the 1908 Olympics. Tommy was a generous host and became well known for his lavish house parties. He was a great patron of 20th-century art and had a lifelong passion for all things medieval. He staged jousts, turned the conservatory into a Hawk House, and lined the Long Gallery with medieval suits of armour. The artist Augustus John once came down to breakfast to find Tommy sitting in an armchair in full armour! In 1946, Tommy left Chirk and retired to his Scottish estates, dying that same year. His legacy lives on in the art, literature, theatre and much else that he supported during his rich and generous life.

Lieutenant-Colonel Ririd and Lady Margaret Myddelton

In 1949, Chirk Castle was once again home to the Myddelton family, with Lieutenant-Colonel Ririd (1902–88) and Lady Margaret Myddelton at the helm. During the war years, the grounds and gardens had been neglected and the couple's primary task was restoration. Many of Pugin's medieval features were stripped out and the neoclassical State Rooms revived. But the Myddeltons couldn't ignore spiralling running costs, nor the fact that the Castle needed more than a lick of paint. While grants had helped tackle deathwatch beetle

Left Thomas Scott-Ellis in full armour, *c.*1925

and dry rot, the Castle was still using, for example, 1912 electrical wiring. Like Richard Myddelton before them, Ririd and Margaret opened the Castle to the public. The income paid for small repairs, but more needed to be done.

Last in line: Guy Myddelton

Ririd passed the Castle and 190 hectares (468 acres) to the state in 1978, after which large-scale repairs were paid through the National Land Fund. Three years later, Chirk was handed to the National Trust and in 2004 Guy Myddelton (born 1966), the Lieutenant-Colonel's grandson, moved out. Guy now lives close by and manages a 1,000-hectare (2,500-acre) agricultural estate. The Myddeltons remain closely linked in other ways, too. A third of the collection is on long-term loan from the family, while Guy and his family keep rooms in the Bachelor's Tower. Chirk Castle may be a medieval castle with a fascinating 700-year history, but to the Myddeltons it was – and still is – a place that tells the story of their family.

Above The children of Ririd and Margaret Myddelton, David, Fiona and Hugh in the entrance archway

Exploring the Castle

Chirk Castle is remarkable for the simple fact that it has been lived in continuously ever since it was built over 700 years ago. Each successive generation has made its mark here.

Layers of history

Exploring the Castle today is like walking through time. In the ancient Adam's Tower, you can sense the harshness of medieval life. The Cromwell Hall chatters with Victorian values. In the East Range, the echoes of grand post-war parties still resonate. And wherever you are, there are traces of the people who lived, worked and died at Chirk during its long history.

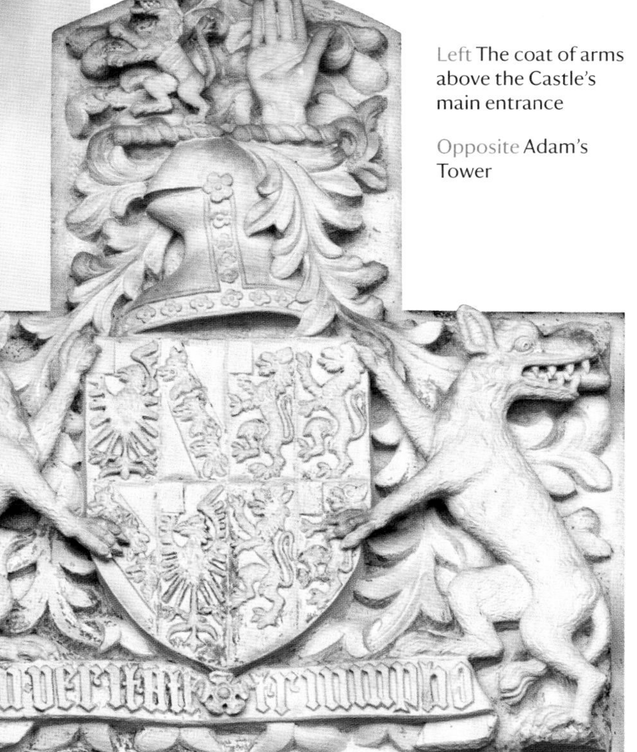

Left The coat of arms above the Castle's main entrance

Opposite Adam's Tower

Stepping in

Crossing a 17th-century stone bridge, you enter the Castle through a surprisingly modest arch. Above it is the Myddelton Biddulph coat of arms, possibly designed by Pugin in the 19th century. The four connected ranges around the courtyard all date from different periods. We begin in the oldest: the West Range.

Timekeeper

The clock tower is a later addition, built in 1609, and the clock and belfry were installed as part of Pugin's work on the Castle in the 19th century. Remarkably for an outdoor clock of its age, it still chimes.

'One of the joys of being here is seeing the different influences of each generation on the Castle. The first Sir Thomas was perhaps the most important member of the Myddelton family in that respect, but each generation has had something to do or say, made some impression. History is like a patchwork here.'

Guy Myddelton, 2013

The West Range

The only medieval part of the Castle to survive, the West Range offers a glimpse of life in one of Edward I's Marcher fortresses. The 14th-century inhabitants lived in the towers, as the curtain walls connecting them were too narrow for anything other than passageways or very small rooms.

Built for defence

Adam's Tower's five-metre-thick walls were highly effective against battering rams. Elsewhere, arrow slit windows, and a 'killing zone' at the entrance comprising a double portcullis and concealed 'murder holes' through which hot liquids could be poured, helped make this an easily defendable castle. In its early years Chirk had a garrison of only about 25 men. What it lacked in manpower, it made up for with clever design.

Down in the dungeon

The ground floor of Adam's Tower is taken up with the guardroom and weapon store. A spiral staircase leads down to the dungeon. Hollowed out of rock, this features two levels. More fortunate prisoners were placed in the Lower Guard with its small, high window and a fireplace. Others were confined in the room below, which has no natural light, ventilation or heating.

Right The Castle's west elevation

Fortress, first and foremost

Chirk was never planned as a family home. This was a military site, important enough for King Edward I to visit during its construction in 1295. The king may well have lent Roger Mortimer the money to build Chirk and possibly even suggested James of St George, the master-builder of Harlech, Beaumaris, Caernarfon and Conwy castles.

The Muniment Room and Sir Thomas's Chamber

Climb the stone stairs from the courtyard door and you reach the Muniment Room, which provided living and working space for senior staff. The higher your rank, the higher up Adam's Tower you went. The rooms on the second floor were occupied by the Castle's governor or owner.

In 1631, the main room was recorded as 'Sir Thomas his owne chamber' – it was here that the first Sir Thomas Myddelton lived after he had handed Chirk to his son. A contemporary inventory describes how the room was laid out, the bare walls softened by tapestries, furniture and Thomas's 'great bedstead'. Little has changed since, apart from the medieval-style fireplace added by Lord Howard de Walden in the 20th century.

Above Arched chambers in Adam's Tower

Right A guard fires an arrow from the battlements as part of a Living History event at Chirk

Magistrate's Court

This narrow room within the curtain wall takes its name from the early 17th-century plasterwork frieze on the wall. Note the figure of a blind and barefoot magistrate holding a set of scales and the sword of justice. It's not entirely clear what the room was used for. If it did act as a court, it was only to settle tenant-related disputes. The red hand on the frieze is the symbol of knighthood adopted by the Myddelton family when Charles II gave them a baronetcy in 1660.

The North Range

The North Range was built in the early 17th century by Sir Thomas Myddelton I, the first owner of Chirk to turn the Castle into a family home. This wing contains a curious mix of the medieval and the classical, although not all is as old as it first appears.

The Cromwell Hall

This room looks like a medieval hall, but it was actually created in the 1840s by A.W.N Pugin, the architect commissioned by Colonel Robert Myddelton to Gothicise the Castle. Pugin brought in the screen, fireplace and heraldry, lights, benches and stained glass; the clock was made from a 16th-century cupboard, the muskets arranged by the architect. What you see today is a Victorian interpretation of how the Great Hall, once the heart of medieval Chirk, would have looked.

Classic before Gothic

The Cromwell Hall has experienced several incarnations. In the early 17th century, servants ate here, with food and beer served through a hatch in the Screens Passage from the Butler's Pantry beyond. After it was usurped by the present Servants' Hall, the space became a grand entrance hall, its neoclassical style 'ornamented with pillars, and floored with white stone, cut in the figure of diamonds, which are intermixed with squares of black marble', as noted a visitor in 1808. Pugin swept the classical away and introduced dark wood panelling, heavy oak furniture and a profusion

Opposite top Five-sided oak buffet or 'court cupboard' with carved bulbous supports, *c.*1600

Opposite below Watercolour of the Cromwell Hall (1862)

Right Gasolier designed by Pugin

Below This heraldic stained glass in the mullioned windows of the Cromwell Hall was installed by Pugin

of heraldry. Later, and up until the Second World War, the Hall was used as a billiard room. Today it is the Castle's only room where Pugin's Victorian design has survived almost intact.

Arms and armour

The Cromwell Hall takes its name from the Civil War armour and muskets that line its walls. There are 38 muskets, the largest such collection outside the Royal Armories. Most were collected by the second Thomas Myddelton, the war general displaying them as a reminder of his success on both sides of England's protracted civil war.

Early treasures and later measures

Although Pugin happily made new fixtures and fittings, he was also fond of 'up-cycling' existing furniture. The two oak armchairs, for instance, date from the James I period, but the carved cresting was added by Pugin. The two five-sided oak buffets are late 16th or early 17th century, but the oak bench was made to Pugin's design. The clock was probably created by Pugin using old materials; its front panel, dated 1689 with the mysterious initials H.R.M., is likely to have been part of a cupboard. Pugin also designed the brass gasolier, which was supplied by Chirk's own gas works built near Home Farm in 1857.

Design variety

As you walk from the Cromwell Hall to the Grand Staircase, you experience two very different styles: Pugin's Victorian Gothic and Joseph Turner's neoclassical. This is more than a simple design clash: the rooms actually 'confuse' the timeline of the Castle. The older-looking Cromwell Hall is in fact more recent than the Grand Staircase. Confusion arises elsewhere in the Castle, particularly where the style of one room was rubbed out by another, only to be overwritten in the original style later on. The State Rooms are a prime example. Created in a neoclassical style in the 1770s, they were Gothicised by Pugin in the 1840s and then returned to their classical elegance in the 1950s.

Classical man

The leading architect of his generation in this part of England, Joseph Turner was brought in by Elizabeth Rushout to transform Chirk Castle into a fashionable country home. In 1766, he was asked to create the State Rooms. An ambitious project, it involved excavating the five-metre-thick walls of the original tower on the north front of the Castle and creating a cantilevered stone staircase within. Turner, who was influenced by the great neoclassical architect and interior designer Robert Adam, introduced elaborate Grecian plasterwork throughout the State Rooms, and removed the dark 17th-century wainscoting. The end result was gloriously elegant and completely at odds with what was to follow.

Above Detail of the fireplace in the Bow Drawing Room

Medieval makers

The 're-medievalisation' of Chirk occurred first via Thomas Harrison and then through Pugin and his friend and collaborator, John Gregory Crace. Thomas Harrison was commissioned in 1820 to transform the East Range, which he did by enclosing the colonnade and adding vaulted ceilings and a corridor to the courtyard front. Pugin's three-year commission, begun in 1846, was far more extensive. There was hardly a

wall, floor, ceiling or piece of furniture he didn't alter. This style tapped into the Victorian trend for romanticising our pre-industrial past, which was a little ironic, given the harsh reality of medieval life. Regardless, Pugin and Crace repainted Turner's neoclassical State Rooms, turning Turner's elegant colour scheme into one that was defiantly High Victorian, with deep reds, flock greens, brown and gold. It was a costly affair. The first phase was completed in 1847 to the tune of £2,650. When Pugin died unexpectedly, his son completed the commission, and when Richard Myddleton inherited in 1872 he too continued the work. This style, so popular with the Victorians, fell completely out of favour in the early 20th century and almost all of it was subsequently cleared away.

Above Neoclassical detail on the Dining Room ceiling

Right Detail of the pelmet in the Saloon made from a Pugin-designed fabric

The State Rooms

The Grand Staircase

Contrasting with Pugin's neo-Gothic fantasy in the Cromwell Room, this elegantly neoclassical space was constructed in 1777–8 by Joseph Turner to replace the 17th-century wooden stairs. Although Turner was influenced by Robert Adam, the garlands and roundels around the ceiling and the four Ionic columns are a nod to Adam's rival, James Wyatt. Amongst the portraits and paintings that hang here are two fine landscape views of the Castle. One, of about 1715 by John Wootton, depicts a stag hunt in the park. The other, by his contemporary Peter Tillemans, includes a view of the Davies Gates before they were moved in 1770.

Peter Tillemans

Chirk features a collection of paintings by the famous painter Peter Tillemans (1684–1734). Born in Antwerp, Tillemans trained there with minor landscape painters before moving to England in 1708 where he started work as a copyist of Old Master painters. He soon became known for the quality and versatility of his art and was employed by the aristocracy to paint genre, history, battle and sporting scenes, as well as portrait groups, landscapes and country house views. The collection at Chirk – which comprises a battle, a landscape and portraits – gives a good idea of the range of Tillemans' work.

London's first clean water

The first Sir Thomas Myddelton was made Lord Mayor of London in 1613. His portrait hangs on the stairwell and depicts him dressed in full mayoral garb. Close by is his brother, Sir Hugh Myddelton. Hugh founded the New River Company, and at the foot of the stairs is a remnant of the company's crowning achievement: an eight-foot elm and yew section of a pipe designed to carry London's first clean water supply. Sir Hugh was a self-taught engineer, his company named after his 'New River', a 38-mile pipeline stretching from the River Lea in Hertfordshire to New River Head in London. It encountered financial difficulties and opposition from landowners from the start. However when King James agreed to pay half the cost in return for a 50% share in the scheme, criticisms stopped and the New River was completed by 1613. Sir Hugh amassed a fortune from silver and lead mines in Wales and was rewarded for the New River, a baronetcy in 1622 and by having places named after him, including Myddelton Square and Myddelton Passage in London. There is a memorial to Sir Hugh on Islington Green, while the New River itself survives and is still partly in use; you can walk its length today along the New River Walk in Canonbury, London.

The State Dining Room

A drawing room, a parlour, a place to eat family meals and finally an 18th-century dining room used to entertain: this space has had many uses over the years. In 1631 it was merely 'the chamber over the buttery' but under Joseph Turner it took on a far grander role. As in the other State Rooms, the moulded plasterwork on the ceiling is in the style of Robert Adam. Pugin painted it to resemble dark oak panelling with reliefs picked out in gold, but after an outbreak of dry rot the Myddeltons repainted it in 1963. The fireplace is 18th-century neoclassical, but was actually bought by Lord Howard de Walden in the 1930s and installed on condition that it should remain when his tenancy expired.

Perfect hosts

Tommy Scott-Ellis, 8th Lord Howard de Walden, and his wife Margherita hosted glittering house parties in the 1930s. Their guest lists read like a who's who of the 20th century's most brilliant minds: Rudyard Kipling, George Bernard Shaw, Hilaire Belloc, Augustus John and a stream of musicians and actors.

Today, the table is set out as if to receive such luminous guests, with 18th-century Bohemian glasses, glassware displaying the crest of the Myddelton baronetcy and a fine mid-19th-century faience dinner service from Strasbourg. Above shines a 19th-century chandelier, which belonged to Lady Margaret Myddelton's stepfather.

'The Howard de Waldens entertained on a large scale, frequently including Royalty among their guests. Mrs Hardy [the cook] was in her element when serving her wonderful meals, full of flavour, colour and attraction on the lovely silver dishes.'

Hilda Wright, First Kitchenmaid from 1935 to 1941

Opposite The State Dining Room

Left During the de Waldens' time Chirk Castle was both a family home and a social centre. Its convivial and relaxed atmosphere is evocatively depicted in this painting by John Lavery: *The Howard de Walden family in the Saloon at Chirk Castle*

The Saloon

This was the location of the first Sir Thomas's Great Parlour and in the 17th century the main dining room. It was once dominated by plaster panels, their fretwork so intricate and heavy that it threatened to come away, bringing the ceiling down with it. Throughout the 1700s attempts were made to repair the panels but in 1770 there was little choice but to pull them down. By this time, Richard Myddelton had decided to turn the room into a Saloon, a fashionable new space in which to entertain guests. The Saloon was also designed to display Richard and his wife Elizabeth's collection of furniture, tapestries and paintings.

Melting pot

Today's interior is, as elsewhere, a curious mix of Turner's neoclassic style and Pugin's neo-Gothic. Turner's ceiling features scenes from Greek mythology painted by the Irish landscapist George Mullins. The deep blue background and gilding were added by Pugin and John Crace, who also covered the walls in flock wallpaper in shades of green, brown and gold. Pugin's alterations were controversial even at the time. In 1855 a visitor from the Shrewsbury Archaeological Institute expressed horror at the colours and by the 1920s, the Howard de Waldens had toned down the scheme to a dull gold.

Above The Saloon

Opposite top Marble chimneypiece flanked by giltwood torchères on tripod stands

Opposite far right Detail of the 'The Building of Thebes', one of four Mortlake tapestries that represent scenes from the story of Cadmus, King of Thebes

Opposite right Detail of the Saloon ceiling of 1772–3

Key works

The furniture and furnishings in this room – from the Japanese inlaid and lacquered cabinets to the tapestries and portraits – are among the best in the Castle. The giltwood pier-glasses dating from 1782, were made using the largest, and hence most expensive, plate glass that could be produced at the time. They originally faced each other at opposite ends of the room and would reflect light back from the candles placed on the pier-tables at night.

Elizabeth's oak and walnut harpsichord was made in 1742 by Burkat Shudi, one of the finest London makers of the period. It is the earliest signed and dated harpsichord in existence and has been restored to playing condition.

The four Mortlake tapestries tell the story of Cadmus, King of Thebes, and were probably bought by the second Sir Thomas Myddelton, while the Axminster carpet was designed by William Morris in 1879 for St James's Palace and is on loan from Her Majesty the Queen.

The Drawing Room

This third and final room of Turner's design was once a 17th-century drawing room as dark as the Long Gallery. The architect ripped out its floor-to-ceiling wainscoting and replaced it with an Adam-style plasterwork ceiling by a Mr Kilminster. Turner also rearranged the windows to give better views over Richard Myddelton's new Pleasure Ground (see page 49).

A long and expensive task

Beginning in the 1770s, the work took 25 years to complete. Myddelton's enormous programme of modernisation was expensive. Spiralling costs forced him to bring the project to a halt halfway through, at least until his finances recovered. When Sir Christopher Sykes visited in 1796 he noted that work was still in progress. He also applauded the fact that the interiors were 'very Magnificent, &

Above A watercolour of the Drawing Room 1862

Opposite top Detail of the blue and gold ceiling decoration, based on Adam designs and produced by Mr Kilminster in 1773

strikingly singular, so not gaudy grand and fine as Alnwick Castle, but more simple'. In Pugin's time, this room became known as the Red Drawing Room because of the 'Crimson Plush' wallpaper he introduced. The grate, fireback and fire-irons are all by Pugin and although they have remained in the room until now, Robert Myddelton Biddulph was less than happy with the result. 'I have now had a fair trial of one of the grates you made me,' he wrote to Pugin in 1847. 'I feel it gives little heat to the fuel it consumes … nor do I see how it can be otherwise, from its shape and construction.'

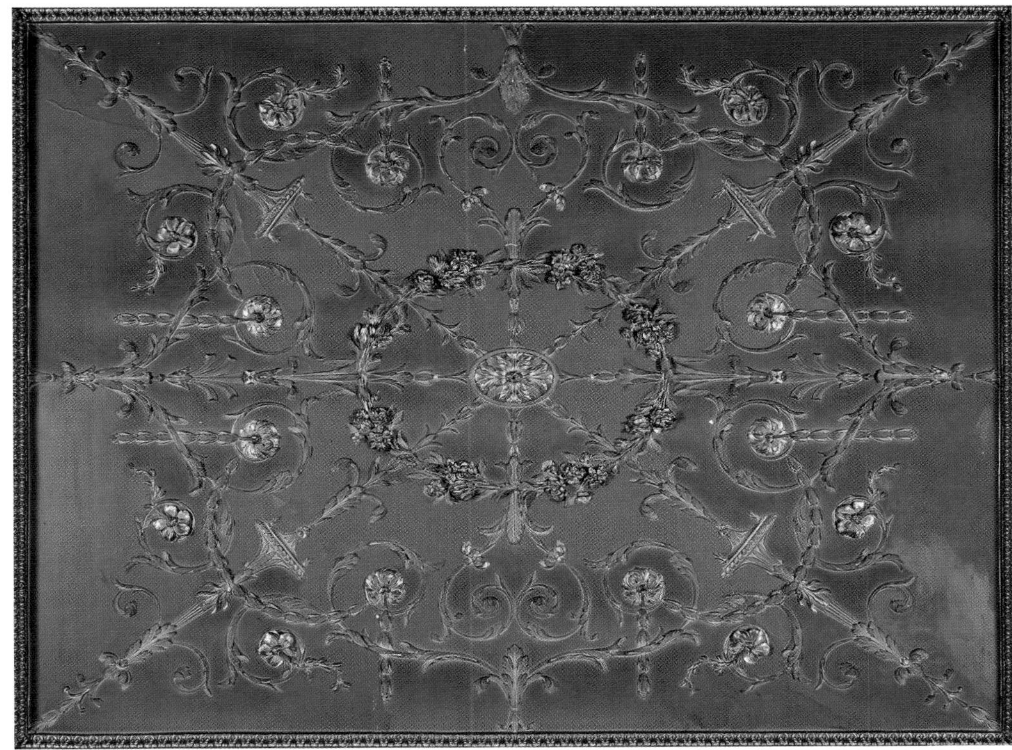

Family portraits
The Drawing Room has long been a place to display family portraits and in 1911, before the Myddeltons' first major sale, it contained over 40 pictures. To visitors, it was known simply as the Picture Gallery. Today, its paintings include two of Richard Myddelton and his wife, Elizabeth by Francis Cotes, and rare portraits of Richard's aunts, Mary and Anne, painted by Peter Tillemans in 1722.

Above The Long Gallery

The Long Gallery

This imposing 30-metre room fills the whole length of the East Range. It was rebuilt by Sir Thomas Myddelton IV, following the devastation of the Civil War. Long galleries were no longer fashionable when Sir Thomas rebuilt his in 1670–8, but it was a practical and economic way of filling a gap in the Castle's demolished walls. Although this type of room was dated, the decoration was not. The scrolled and swagged oak panelling was probably created by the celebrated country house architect Captain William Winde and the furniture, metalwork and pictures were brought from London to replace that which had been plundered during the Civil War. When complete, the Long Gallery carried a clear message: the Myddeltons were back in business. Later additions include the 18th-century Rococo fireplaces, Pugin's 1840s ribbed ceiling and Minton tiles bearing the MB monogram for Myddelton Biddulph.

Right 17th-century Dutch ebony cabinet, inlaid with tortoiseshell and ivory, with painted scenes from the studio of Frans Francken the Younger

A multi-purpose space

The Long Gallery was originally designed as a space for gentle exercise, where one could walk and look at portraits of family members and friends. In 1686, a billiard table was recorded here and was still present in the 1840s, after which the room became much more crowded. The Victorians filled it with furniture and curiosities – including a stuffed leopard on castors – and Lord Howard de Walden lined it with suits of armour. In the main, however, the Long Gallery continued to be used for parties, games, dances and billiards and, as originally, for exercise. Guy Myddelton remembers learning to ride a bike here as a child.

Treasures of the Long Gallery

The Long Gallery contains some important pieces. Dating from about 1600, the Japanese sharkskin (shagreen) chest opens to show a black lacquered interior decorated with a mother-of-pearl panther. It probably belonged to the first Sir Thomas Myddelton. He helped fund the exploits of Sir Francis Drake and Sir Walter Raleigh and in so doing secured a share of the wealth from Spanish ships they plundered. Whether this chest came from such a ship or was simply an item he came across during his time at the East India Company, we will never know. We can be sure however that the silks and spices contained within the chest were much more valuable than the piece of furniture itself.

The 17th-century Dutch ebony cabinet was a gift from King Charles II to Sir Thomas Myddelton III in 1661. Inlaid with tortoiseshell and ivory, the double doors and internal drop front show scenes from the life of Christ. They were painted on copper panels in the Antwerp studio of Frans Francken the Younger, and are surrounded by delicate silver metalwork. Inside are secret compartments and hidden drawers – perfect for keeping precious items away from prying eyes.

The King's Bedroom

Charles I spent two nights at Chirk during the Civil War, hence the name of this room. At the time, in 1645, Sir Thomas III was a confirmed Parliamentarian and his Castle was held by Royalist forces. It is unlikely that Charles actually slept in this room as this part of the Castle was demolished and rebuilt after the war. Much else in the King's Bedroom is from a later period too: the ceiling was probably based on a design by Pugin, while the fireplace was supplied by him and the woodwork painted to his specification. The National Trust has restored this room to its 19th-century appearance, adding for instance the reproduction flock wallpaper.

Opposite The State Bed with its crimson silk damask hangings and ornately carved footboard

Right Carved wooden figure from the old Chapel ceiling

Bed of lies

The State Bed bears an inscription on its silvered footboard that proudly declares it was slept in by Charles I – but this is not true. The frame wasn't made until about 1700 (50 years after his execution) and it came to Chirk from Wanstead, the Essex home of Elizabeth Rushout. The footboard itself is likely to be a 19th-century addition. The bed was sold during the 1911 sale and bought for St Donat's Castle in South Glamorgan, but was sold again. Much later, it was discovered by chance and bought back for Chirk by Colonel Ririd Myddelton.

The Chapel

There has been a chapel at Chirk since at least 1329, but the present one dates from the mid-15th century. Unfortunately, the 17th-century wood fittings, including a grand carved and gilded organ and case ordered by the second Sir Thomas Myddelton, have all gone. The fourth Sir Thomas introduced a pulpit, altar, gallery and pews, but these too had disappeared by the 18th century when the Chapel fell into disrepair. It was restored in the 19th century, with final alterations carried out by Lord Howard de Walden in 1912; his is the oak floor and panelling, the fireplace, carved overmantel, and the galleried stair passage connecting the Long Gallery with the South Range.

The East Range

The East Range is a later addition and contains private family apartments commissioned by Charlotte Myddelton Biddulph and her husband Robert. This wing remained a home for the Myddeltons until Guy and his family moved out in 2004, and has since been restored by the Trust to show what life at Chirk was like under the Howard de Waldens.

The Pugin Corridor

Although Thomas Harrison built this wing in a medieval style in the 1820s, Pugin created the Gothic façade, with this corridor a mish-mash of both men's designs. The doors and doorframes are, for example, probably Harrison's, whereas the door plates and locks were added by Pugin. You'll notice how the locks are not a perfect fit. This was a deliberate ploy by Pugin to create the impression that they had been added to original medieval doors. A painting by Mary Wombwell, daughter of Robert and Fanny Myddelton Biddulph, depicts the corridor in 1862. It shows Harrison's ceiling grained so that it appeared as dark oak, and with added shoulder-height wainscoting. The painting also shows a stone-flagged floor; the present one dates from the late 19th century when the Myddeltons began stripping out Pugin's interiors.

Opposite The view along the Pugin Corridor

God's own architect

The architect, writer and designer Augustus Welby Northmore Pugin (1812–52) is a major figure in the history of 19th-century architecture and decorative arts – and it is partly to him that we owe the Gothic Revival. His passion for medieval architecture led Pugin to study and sketch buildings in Northern Europe and across Britain, becoming an expert in 14th- and 15th-century buildings.

In 1835 he converted to Catholicism and his faith became the driving force behind his ideas on design and architecture. He fervently believed that 'Christian architecture', as he called it, had the power to influence the spirit and had a moral role to play. Not content with just designing churches, he applied his vision to the whole field of design, working on stained glass, metalwork, furniture, textiles, wallpapers, ceramics and jewellery.

He famously worked on the interiors of the Houses of Parliament, for which he designed all the fittings and furnishings, including carvings, giltwork, panelling, furniture and even the doorknobs. Some experts believe that he designed Big Ben and played a key role in the architecture of the Houses of Parliament.

The Library

Chirk Castle's library has had many locations over the centuries. When the brothers Robert and John Myddelton inherited, they brought with them a serious book collection – and talk started of creating a dedicated library to house it. Thomas Harrison's 1820 plans show the library at the top of the Bachelor's Tower. Pugin described ideas for a library, but it is unclear whether he went any further. It was Richard Myddelton who created the Library as we know it, with Lord Howard de Walden continuing to use it well into the 20th century. When the Myddeltons moved out in 2004, the family sold many of its books, but over 80 per cent were bought back by the Trust and returned to the shelves. The Myddeltons were a well-read family, with books collected continually over the years – complete libraries such as these are rare. The Library reveals the changing tastes, interests and intellectual pursuits of a noble Welsh family over the centuries. Later, the Victorian era saw a fashion for rebinding whole libraries; thankfully this trend was resisted at Chirk, and so its books tell the long story of English and Welsh bookbinding.

Far left Neo-Gothic chair in the Library

Left Items on one of the Library tables

A Bible for Wales
The most important item in the Library is Sir Thomas's copy of Y Beibl Bach. The printing of this popular Welsh edition of the Bible, pocket-sized and published in 1630, was partly paid for by Sir Thomas. By dint of its size and affordability, it is credited with helping keep the Welsh language alive as it brought the written form of the language into thousands of ordinary Welsh homes.

Y BIBL
CYSSEGR-LAN,
SEF YR HEN
DESTAMENT
A'R NEWYDD.

2 TIM. 3. 16, 17.

Printiedig yn LLUNDAIN gan
ROBERT BARKER Printiwr i
Ardderchoccaf fawrhydi y Brenin : a chan Assignes IOHN BILL.
Anno Dom [illegible]

Opposite top The Library

Opposite below Detail of the carved 19th-century bookcases

The Lower Dining Room

Once the family's dining room, after the de Waldens rented the Castle this was for many years a schoolroom, only reverting to its original use during the Second World War. Today, it is designed to feel like a family room – visitors are welcome to sit at the table and make themselves at home. On the wall hangs the Myddelton Pedigree. It proclaims at length the noble past of the family, tracing its family tree from 1670 back to Welsh princes and ancient English kings. The scroll is 10 metres long and was commissioned in around 1660 to mark the baronetcy recently granted by King Charles II. Restored by the Trust in 2012, a different 2-metre stretch is displayed every year, while a replica rests open on the table. On an opposite wall, hangs John Lavery's *The Chess Players* (1929). A depiction of family life at the Castle, it shows Margaret and Pip Scott-Ellis, Lord Howard de Walden's daughters, sitting on the floor playing chess.

The Bow Drawing Room

Another painting by John Lavery shows the Scott-Ellis family in the Saloon in the late 1920s. Again, two girls play chess, their mother is at the piano, 'little Rosemary' leans against an armchair. Tommy, Lord Howard de Walden, talks to his son, while two dogs lie on the floor. It was this picture of domestic bliss that inspired and informed the refurbishment of the Bow Drawing Room.

While there are elements here of earlier inhabitants – Pugin's fireplace has survived and the fan-vaulted ceiling is Harrison's – this room is dedicated to the de Waldens and gives a glimpse into the noise and chatter of this family of seven and their constant stream of illustrious guests. The wireless in the room plays work by Dylan Thomas (whom Tommy supported) as well as an opera co-written by Tommy and the composer Josef Holbrooke.

Below The Bow Drawing Room

Above Looking into the Bow Drawing Room

Right above 1930s wireless in the Bow Drawing Room

Right below Framed photograph of Lord Howard de Walden in First World War uniform

The wireless itself hints at the enquiring mind of a polymath who had a hand in early radio communications, the development of early speedboats and First World War tanks. The guest book is full of the names of society visitors: George Bernard Shaw, Rudyard Kipling, King George and Queen Mary, and many more. On the walls hang portraits by the celebrated artist, Augustus John, of Tommy and Margherita. A bronze bust of Lord Howard by Auguste Rodin sits close by.

Beyond all these wonderful associations and artworks, this room is all about the welcoming atmosphere which was present at Chirk when the de Waldens lived here – so settle down, grab a book and relax in a comfortable armchair.

Welsh arts and culture

Alongside his life-long support of British art, music, opera and drama, Tommy, Lord Howard de Walden, paid special attention to the Welsh arts. His funds allowed the London Symphony Orchestra to tour Wales between the wars. With Augustus John he established the Contemporary Art Society for Wales. He also held an annual competition for new Welsh drama. In 1914, he established the short-lived Welsh National Drama Company, whose achievements include the staging of the first Welsh play, acted in Welsh by professional actors in a 'proper' theatre. He sponsored the publication of Dylan Thomas's first collection of poetry. He also supported the Eisteddfod, the annual national festival of Welsh art, music and performance. Described in 1933 by *The Western Mail* as 'the patron saint of Welsh drama', Tommy paid for the staging of one of the National Eisteddfod's greatest achievements, a performance of *Pob un* (*Everyman*), a translation of the German medieval play *Jedermann*. It was watched by over 10,000 people.

Lord Howard de Walden was not the only resident of Chirk to support Welsh culture. The first Sir Thomas Myddelton paid for the pocket Welsh-language Bible, Y Beibl Bach. And in the Long Gallery, you can hear music from the Chirk part-books. This 16th-century devotional music, which was commissioned by Sir Thomas, had been lost for centuries until the scores reappeared in New York in the 1960s. These part-books were edited by Dr David Evans at the University of Bangor. Today these rare musical works, unique to Chirk Castle, are being performed once again.

Reliving Chirk

Tommy supported many artists, writers and inventors, but he was not averse to coming up with his own ideas as well. In the Ante Room you can perform The Reluctant Dragon, one of six Christmas pantomimes Tommy wrote for his children. To get even more of a taste of what Chirk was like in the 1920s and 1930s, why not watch our cine film, put together as if by Tommy himself, and see original film footage, photographs and quotes from his letters?

Right Cover of the 1933 Eisteddfod programme

Below During the 1922 Harlech historical pageant, Lady Howard de Walden dressed up as Queen Margaret and Tommy as Jasper Tudor (uncle of Henry VII)

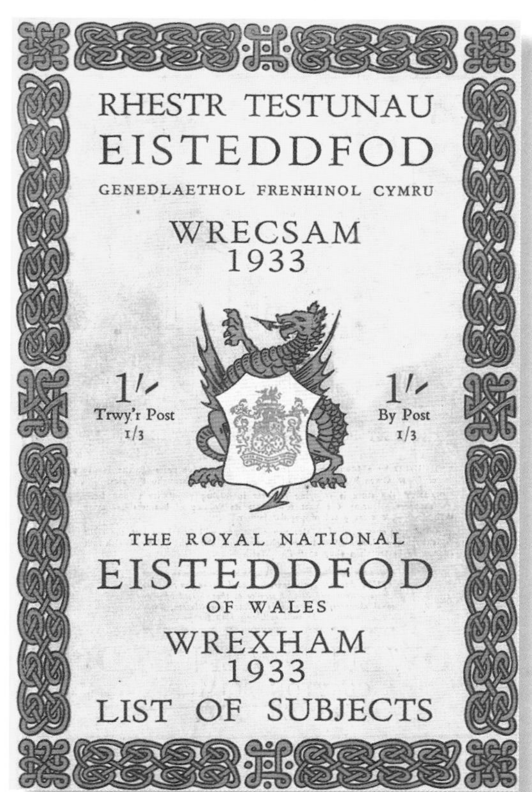
RHESTR TESTUNAU
EISTEDDFOD
GENEDLAETHOL FRENHINOL CYMRU
WRECSAM
1933

1/- Trwy'r Post 1/3

1/- By Post 1/3

THE ROYAL NATIONAL
EISTEDDFOD
OF WALES
WREXHAM
1933
LIST OF SUBJECTS

Strange swords

Tommy's support of Welsh culture sometimes had a practical application. As second-in-command of the 9th Battalion, the Royal Welch Fusiliers on the Western Front in 1916, Tommy noted that the soldiers hadn't been issued with bayonets. So he worked with craftsman Felix Joubert to design a modern version of the cledd, a medieval Welsh short sword. Inscribed Dros Urddas Cymru ('for the honour of Wales'), these swords most definitely saw action. Documents of the time record the fusiliers 'carrying the strange knives furnished by Lord Howard de Walden' in battle. The one in the Bow Drawing Room was Tommy's own.

The South Range

The South Range brings us right back to the 16th century. Under the direction of officials working for Henry VIII, this wing was built as a more habitable alternative to the military quarters that made up the rest of the Castle. A 'great chamber' was constructed on the first floor and arrow slit windows were replaced by mullioned ones.

When the Castle was completed in 1310, it had a South Range, but we know that this wasn't it. At some point after it was built, the original south front collapsed. Henry VIII's men reused the loose masonry to create the South Range that we see today.

The Servants' Hall

This smoke-stained room was built in 1529, and was a dining hall from 1726 until the Second World War. In the 18th century, the 40 or so staff who worked at the Castle took their meals here, their place at the table governed by a

Above The Servants' Hall

Opposite top Costumed interpreter in the Laundry

Opposite below The beer trolley in the Servants' Hall

clearly defined hierarchy and their conduct dictated by the rules hanging over the fireplace. The beer trolley, which was wheeled up and down the room to allow staff to help themselves, was as strictly monitored as the staff. If you misbehaved you could expect to lose part or all of your daily beer allowance.

Much of the furniture here dates back to the 17th and 18th centuries. The carved elm 'Turke and blackeymore' figures were once part of the North Range's 17th-century staircase and probably allude to the first Sir Thomas's connections to the East India Company. The 'tavern' clock was made in 1763 by John Jones of Chester. Many of the movable objects, such as the 18th-century pewter and the leather fire buckets, are either stamped 'Chirk Castle' or marked with the Myddelton hand or the initials of Richard Myddelton – presumably to make sure that nothing went astray.

The Tea Room

Today's Tea Room occupies a space that has long been used to prepare food. It once housed a Tudor range and served the State Dining Room. The original 16th-century staircase leads to the Butler's Pantry above. Its Edwardian sink, the butler's cupboard lined with green baize to protect glassware, the bell board and 1912 telephone all speak of life below stairs. Along a corridor known as the Candle Passage are cupboards pierced with holes; these allowed the smelly, tallow candles of the 16th century to air. Close by is a linen closet. Daily tours explain how this area of the house was used to help run such a large family home.

The Laundry

Originally a bothy on the far side of the garden, the Laundry moved to behind the South Range in 1790 and was in use up until the Second World War. It was restored and re-opened to the public in 2006. Today you can listen to recordings of former laundry maids from the 1930s as they talk about their work here.

The Garden

Covering 2.2 hectares (5.5 acres), the garden at Chirk is peaceful, unexpected, and a triumph. The second highest in Britain, it offers views that stretch across valleys, hills and counties. With its immaculate lawns, neatly trimmed topiary, ancient trees, rose garden, wooded pleasure ground, artistic statues and unusual Hawk House, the garden is arguably as impressive as the Castle itself.

Supporting the community

Sir Thomas II's new garden was a way of creating work for locals who had been battered by war. In this poem, he acknowledged the scale of his scheme and explained how it brought wider benefits.

When first, I did begin, to make
This Garden, I did undertake,
A Worke, I knew not when begun,
What it would Cost, ere it was donn,
But I repent not, for ye poore,
Doe there finde worke; had none before.

I found some worke for every trade,
Some walles did make, some Arbours made,
Some mowed ye Allys, some I putt,
To preuine ye vines, and Hedges cutt,
And some poore weomen, that had neede,
I kept, & payd them, for to weede.

A potted history

Sir Thomas Myddelton II laid out a formal garden in 1653, following contemporary French examples. He may have been making a political point: the style he chose was one likely to have been enjoyed by King Charles II, who at the time was exiled in France and to whom Sir Thomas had transferred his allegiance.

The next major influence was Richard Myddelton. In 1764 he commissioned landscape architect William Emes to undertake an ambitious remodelling of the park and gardens. Although Emes kept many elements of the existing formal garden, beyond its boundaries he moved fences, walls and even the drovers' paths in front of the Castle, planted thousands of trees, introduced sweeping lawns and installed a ha-ha to open up views. He also created a new approach to the Castle.

In the 19th century, yew topiary, hedges and wrought-iron gates were introduced. Then, under the guidance of Lord Howard de Walden, the celebrated gardener Norah Lindsay created a magnificent herbaceous border on the Upper Lawn. After the Second World War, Lady Margaret Myddelton skilfully and almost single-handedly revived the by now neglected gardens, creating the colourful planting schemes we still see today, including the borders along the east wall of the Castle and on the Upper Lawn.

Opposite In the winter months, the garden's structure of yew hedges and topiary stands out

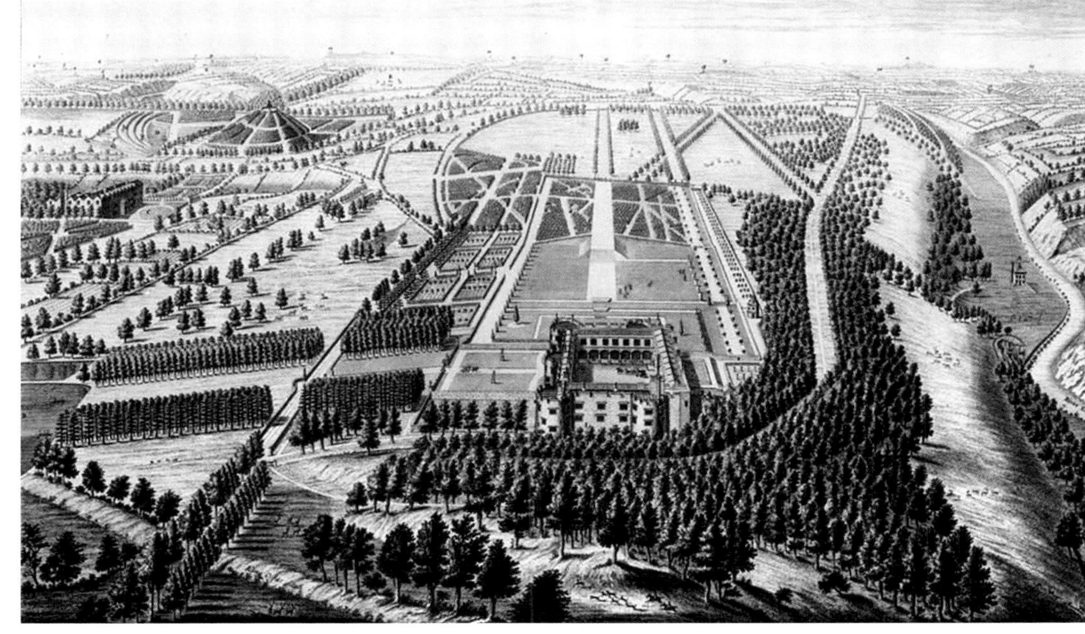

Below This 1735 bird's-eye sketch of Chirk by Thomas Badeslade shows terraced lawns, a bowling green, a kitchen garden and tree-lined avenues

The mystery of Mars

Like the Castle, the garden has its intriguing stories. One tale relates to the lead statue of Hercules, which now stands at the head of the Lime Avenue. Made in 1720, it originally stood at one end of the Davies Gates. On the other side was a companion statue depicting Mars. Impressive as they undoubtedly were, they were nevertheless moved by William Emes into outlying woods and for about 200 years remained out of sight and out of mind. At some point, Hercules fell off his plinth and rolled into scrub; he was eventually rediscovered (minus a hand) and the decision was made to restore him. To get him to the Lime Avenue, he had to be winched across the landscape by helicopter. Mars has never been found. Maybe some day he will be discovered.

Bronze beauties

Elsewhere in the gardens are four Art Nouveau bronze nymphs by the Anglo-Italian Andrea Carlo Lucchesi bought by the Howard de Waldens. Lucchesi was an exponent of the late 19th-century 'New Sculpture' movement which asked for greater naturalism in art and a move away from contemporary neoclassical 'blandness'. Sir Frederick Leighton is acknowledged as having started the movement when he exhibited his powerfully striking and dynamic *An Athlete Wrestling with a Python* at the Royal Academy in 1877.

The challenge of Chirk

The garden is located 210 metres above sea level. The soil is poor and light, the winds strong and relentless. From its earliest days, Chirk gardeners have planted trees to act as shelter and for centuries this plan worked. But in the 1940s, a significant number of decaying 17th-century oaks had to be felled, and the garden was once again exposed. The solution has been the gradual replanting of the Garden Wood, followed by a slow and on-going reintroduction of tender trees and shrubs.

Opposite top and bottom Views of the restored Hercules statue

Above Art Nouveau sculpture by Andrea Carlo Lucchesi in the Shrub Garden

Right Two nymphs frame the view towards the Hawk House

Garden highlights

The main entrance to the garden is through the **Screen**, the remains of the enormous iron gate that once marked the north entrance to the Castle and included the Davies Gates. To the right are the **Castle Borders**. The Bachelor's Tower is softened by an enormous climbing *Hydrangea petiolaris*.

No one leaves Chirk Castle without commenting on its **yew topiary**, introduced in 1872 by Richard Myddelton Biddulph. A stickler for precise pruning, he would demand a recut if their annual trim fell short of his exacting standards. It takes six weeks to cut the hedges at Chirk – no mean feat when you consider that the garden is looked after by just three full-time gardeners. The hedges, incidentally, are important to the lesser horseshoe bats that live in the Laundry; they use the distinct shapes to navigate when flying to and from their colony. The **Formal Garden** is dominated by a towering 'crown on a cushion' yew topiary.

The **Rose Garden** was planted by Richard's artistically minded son, Algernon. Its cherub was a gift to Lady Margaret Myddelton from her stepfather, the 1st Lord Astor of Hever.

Above Pruning the climbing hydrangea

Below Looking towards the Upper Lawn

Opposite top The Shrub Garden

Opposite below A spring scene of magnolias and bluebells

The **Upper Lawn** was created by Lady Margaret. A long border on the left follows the gentle slope and is planted in four bays separated by **flowering cherries**. Each bay is related to one of the four seasons. The rough area opposite has a bright display of spring daffodils and is dominated by an **ancient larch** thought to be 250–300 years old. The garden is particularly rich in unusual varieties of tree, from the **Chilean Fire Bush** (*Embothrium coccineum*) found here among the brilliant foliage of various **acers** to the **Handkerchief Tree** (*Davidia involucrata*) in the Shrub Garden, so called because of its large white bracts that appear in mid-May.

The **Hawk House** on the Lower Lawn was originally a conservatory built in the 1850s. Lord Howard de Walden added the thatched roof in about 1912 and used it to house his falcons. Close by, the fragrant, south-facing **Mediterranean Border** is wonderful in late summer. The **Terrace** and, further along, William Emes's **Classical Pavilion** (known as the 'retreat seat') are good places to admire the spectacular view as well as Emes's strategically planted clumps of trees. The quiet, sheltered **Shrub Garden** opposite the Hawk House is an example of Lady Margaret's thrifty approach: many of the plants were given to her by friends and family. Today, the **pond** teems with wildlife, such as emperor dragonflies, diving beetles and great crested newts.

The **Pleasure Ground Wood** is a complete contrast: this wild wood is open every February to show off its incredible display of **snowdrops**, which are in turn followed by **bluebells** and **foxgloves**.

The Estate

Once a sprawling estate of 4,050 hectares (10,000 acres), Chirk Castle's estate today takes in some 195 hectares (480 acres) of woodland, deer park, farmland and a golf course. There has been a hunting forest here as long as there has been a castle.

A winter view from the north west

Right Neoclassical pavilion with ha-ha in the foreground

Below right A Stag Hunt at Chirk Castle by John Wootton (1682-1764)

The park was gradually expanded by successive Myddeltons, and then landscaped as part of William Emes's grand scheme. Because of the estate's 500-strong deer herd, Emes created a sunken ditch, or ha-ha, to stop them from entering the gardens. He also planted thousands of broad-leaved trees, and in 1767 all the roads crossing the park were closed. It was an unpopular decision: the roads included an ancient drovers' path used by farmers to herd cattle to market in Wrexham. Emes's closure added 11 miles to their journey.

The thrill of the chase

The Myddelton family still uses the estate for shooting. The annual shoot, with tens of thousands of pheasants reared every October, is a private affair but occasionally you will see pheasants out on the estate. These are the ones that got away!

Caring for the land

The woods on the wider estate are of vital importance: to the bats who navigate by them, to the rare dead wood beetles who feast on dead branches, and to many other rare and endangered creatures. Over three-quarters of the trees on the estate are oak. There are a number of 'veteran' trees too, all of which are over 400 years old.

The woods are located within an Area of Outstanding Natural Beauty and are also a Site of Special Scientific Interest. The National Trust plays a vital role in looking after this important area. The Deer Shed Wood, for instance, is being replanted with native broad-leaf trees. In the Lower Garden Wood the Trust is trying to restore the ancient pasture woodland, that would have once been commonplace in the medieval era, by introducing wild Welsh ponies.

Working the land

The estate is looked after by a team of just three rangers. Not only are they responsible for planting trees, repairing fences and many other maintenance tasks, but they also work with schools and lead themed walks to share their knowledge. One of their biggest jobs is the removal of non-native trees – such as

Above Welsh ponies

Opposite above Black sheep on the estate

Opposite below The estate's management plan includes the planting of young native trees

Japanese Larch – that have crept onto the estate. These are gradually being replaced with native trees such as oaks, which are in turn interspersed with wildlife-friendly native specimens including crab apple, wild cherry and hazel.

Walking the land

The National Trust has opened up the estate for walkers, first with a woodland walk, whose all-weather surface makes it a buggy-friendly option, and more recently through monthly guided walks that range from bat walks to family trails.

The Veteran Trees Initiative

The estate is part of the national Veteran Trees Initiative, a project to promote the conservation of trees which are of great age and size. The aim is to develop a comprehensive and consistent method of survey for veteran trees. 'The ancient trees across the estate provide a rich habitat for many species and it's vital we look after them so that they're around for years to come,' explains Head Ranger, Carl Green.

Above Dead trees are an important part of the estate, providing food and shelter for rare beetles

Dead wood beetles

Bleached white by the sun and silhouetted against the sky, the estate's dead trees are an arresting sight, yet they are not left there purely for aesthetic effect. One of the reasons why the estate is designated a Site of Special Scientific Interest is that it is one of the richest sites in Wales for saproxylic invertebrates – insects that feed on the dead and dying wood of ancient trees.

A recent survey identified 174 species of beetle and 50 species of fly. Trees are not pruned, unless for safety reasons, and fallen branches are left in situ. The result is a landscape that looks slightly 'untidy', but which many beetles and insects consider home.

Offa's Dyke

Behind Home Farm is a section of the remarkable Offa's Dyke, an 8th-century earthwork built to mark the border between the ancient kingdoms of Mercia and Powys. It runs through the middle of the artificial lake created by William Emes and was a casualty of his uncompromising vision. The remains of the drovers' path that Emes swept away are also still evident as deep depressions in the ground in certain parts of the estate, such as those near Baddy's Park.

Below and right **The highly intricate Davies Gates**

The Davies Gates

These exuberant Baroque gates – now a scheduled monument – were commissioned by Sir Richard Myddelton in 1712 and made by two local blacksmiths, Robert and John Davies, using iron from Richard's forge at Pont-y-blew. They were later supplemented by the screens that are today at the entrance to the garden, and flanked by the statues of Hercules and Mars. William Emes moved the gates in 1770, and they were moved again in 1888, this last time to face the new railway station at Chirk. The gates' incredible detailing includes the Myddleton coat of arms emblazoned with three wolves' heads and the red hand crest of the family.

Home Farm

For many visitors, Home Farm is the very first thing they encounter at Chirk and it's a good place to start exploring. The farm buildings were remodelled in the mid-19th century by Pugin. Today the derelict remains of Pugin's 1857 gasworks, a 16th-century dovecote and the 1930s squash court built by Lord Howard de Walden for his daughters can all be seen behind the farm.

The farm today contains the ticket office, with the former threshing barn now a café and shop selling local produce, meat and game from the estate, as well as vegetables produced in the farm's small kitchen garden. You can buy plants here too, as well as log tables and chairs made from fallen trees on the estate, and slate planters created from unused Chirk slates.

Family fun

During the spring and summer months, Chirk offers lots of family activities. Children can build dens, drive tractors, play tennis, borrow a backpack full of exciting things to do, and lots more!